JJ GOES TO PUPPY CLASS

written by
Diane Rose-Solomon

with
Lyssa Noble Dennis

illustrated by
Lisette Rotman

Acknowledgments

Thank you to my family, especially Andy, Jamie and Zander for your expertise, love and support.

Thank you to Misty Cook for your professional editing and input. You made this book so much better.

Much gratitude to The Women's Council for your love and support once again.

Thank you to Jennifer Fischman for always having my back.

And none of this would be possible without the expert training my dogs and my family have received over the years from Lyssa Noble Dennis and Lynn Medlin.

Printed and bound in China on FSC® Certified paper with soy based inks.

Published by SOP3 Publishing
www.sop3publishing.com

SOP3PUBLISHING.COM

MIX
Paper from
responsible sources
FSC® C008047

Book design by Lisette Rotman

ISBN 978-0-9857690-2-4
LCCN 2014916520

Dedicated to families who take
the time to train their pets
which deepens that loving bond.

We love our puppy JJ so much. My Uncle Jerry found him on a soccer field a month ago but couldn't keep him. That was really lucky for me, because now JJ has a forever home with us.

Mom and Dad weren't too happy about some of the things JJ did right after we got him, but they never got mad. They knew it was all part of being a puppy. Since we really love JJ, we signed him up for puppy class with Trainer Lyssa right away.

Mom said that going to puppy class is like going to school.

In Puppy Class, JJ makes friends with others dogs, like I make friends at school.

JJ also learns basic commands like "Sit," "Down," "Wait," "Stay," "Watch Me," and "Come," just like I learned that red means "stop" and green means "go."

Trainer Lyssa also helped us at home and gave us some great suggestions. Here are some things that happened when JJ first came to live in our house.

One day, I walked into the family room and...

"Uh oh, JJ peed on the carpet! What are we going to do now?"

Trainer Lyssa said, "Puppies need to be walked or let out in the yard every one to two hours to set them up for potty-training success. Praise JJ when he goes where he is supposed to by saying, 'Good Potty!'"

Mom said, "Puppies have to be potty-trained just like you did when you were little. Only he goes potty outside and you use the bathroom."

Another day I turned around and...

"Uh oh, the puppy chewed my favorite stuffed animal! What are we going to do now?"

Trainer Lyssa said, "All puppies love to chew. It's important that JJ has proper toys to play with, like chew bones from the pet store."

Mom said, "Just like you loved your pacifier when you were little."

One day on a walk...

"Uh oh, the puppy pulled Dad on the leash...
what should we do now?"

Trainer Lyssa said, "Keep JJ by your side on a walk with the 'Watch Me' and 'Good Walking' commands, which are both rewarded with treats. She also recommended a no-pull collar to keep JJ from hurting himself.

Mom said, "Just like no one runs ahead when we go out. We stay together to be safe."

Once, when we let JJ outside to go potty...

"Uh oh, JJ dug a hole in the back yard! What are we going to do now?"

Trainer Lyssa said, "It's a good idea to pick a space where your puppy is allowed to dig. Redirect JJ to your preferred spot and say 'Good Dig!' when he digs there."

Mom said, "Just like you're allowed to dig at the beach but you're not allowed to dig up our garden."

One day, a friend came over and JJ got very excited...

"Uh oh, the puppy jumped on my friend! What should we do now?"

Trainer Lyssa said, "Puppies get excited when visitors come to the door. Before you open the door, put JJ on a leash or in his crate to make sure he doesn't jump."

Mom said, "When we see our friends, we don't jump on them. We greet them with hugs even if we are excited."

The other day, when we were out walking JJ, we looked across the street and saw a little boy run right up to a dog he didn't know.

Trainer Lyssa said, "Only pet dogs whose owners tell you it's ok. You should approach the dog in a calm way that says 'let's be friends,' making sure not to look him in the eye. That can be scary for a dog."

Hi Doggie!

Mom said, "Just like we don't sneak up on strangers. Always ask pet parents if it's ok to pet their dogs."

17

One day when I was playing on the floor, I felt a pinch...

"Uh oh, the puppy nipped at my body and hair! What should we do now?"

Trainer Lyssa said, "Puppies really like to use their mouths to play, but it's safer to discourage nipping, especially at children. If it is your turn to play on the floor, you can put JJ behind a baby gate or on a leash attached to a table for a short while."

Mom said, "Just like you like to play with your friends sometimes, and other times you prefer to have quiet time in your room. Puppies need quiet time too."

One day JJ was making a lot of noise...

"Uh oh, the puppy has been barking at all the people and dogs that walk by the house! What should we do now?"

Trainer Lyssa said, "It is natural for dogs to bark. It's their way of communicating. When JJ barks, make a louder sound like slamming a book on a table. This will quiet him. Then praise him for being quiet by saying 'Good Quiet'."

Mom said, "Just like you learned to use your indoor voice."

One day, on a long walk...

"Uh Oh, JJ wants to run across the street! What should we do now?"

Trainer Lyssa said, "Remember, a grown up should always walk your puppy on a leash and enforce the 'Wait' command at corners.

When a grown-up has made sure no cars are coming and it is safe to cross, say 'OK' to JJ before you cross the street together."

Mom said, "Just like when I hold your hand to cross the street."

One day, when we were leaving the house...

"Uh oh, JJ tried to run out the front door! What should we do now?"

Trainer Lyssa said, "When you leave the house, you should put JJ behind a baby gate or in his crate. When he is a little older, you can use the 'Wait' command or toss treats for him to chase away from the door."

Mom said, "Just like when you look out the window at school and it makes you want to run and play outside."

Yesterday, we noticed our fluffy puppy on the living room sofa.

"Uh oh, JJ jumped on the furniture! What should we do now?"

Trainer Lyssa said, "Every family has different rules about allowing pets on the furniture. You can try putting hangers or aluminum foil on the furniture you don't want JJ to touch. He won't want to sit on them and will eventually learn to stay away."

Mom said, "Just like you learned to keep your shoes off the sofa, the puppy is learning the rules of the house."

One day, I went into the laundry room and...

"Uh Oh, the puppy got into the kitty litter box again! What should we do now?"

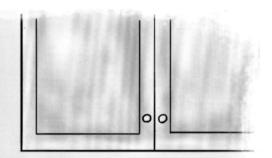

Trainer Lyssa said, "Cat poop and cat food are very appealing to dogs but not very good for their bellies. Keep the litter box and cat food in a place where the cat can reach, but JJ can't."

Mom said, "Just like we eat healthy foods like fruits and veggies, but we avoid foods that aren't good for our bellies."

Yippee! JJ licks my face, plays catch, follows me around the house and snuggles with me at rest time. When he sits, or waits, or watches me, I tell him "Good Dog" so that he keeps learning exactly what he's supposed to do.

Even though he still does a lot of silly puppy things and didn't learn everything I showed him right away, JJ is already my best friend.

Author's note:

Remember, the puppy stage doesn't last forever. It can be frustrating but it is also a very sweet time. This book is not a substitute for professional dog training. My intention is to introduce young children to the idea of patience during basic puppy training.

Did you know that dogs can learn over 200 words? There is no reason to say "no" over and over again or be frustrated when your dog doesn't do what you say. Adults should find a quality obedience class that teaches basic commands and properly socializes your dog with positive training techniques. With a little time and dedication, you will have him behaving the way you expect in your home. More importantly, you'll discover unconditional love, companionship, and a dedicated friend for life. Some families prefer private dog training lessons to group training lessons. Either way, any time spent training your pup and practicing in between classes strengthens your bond.

While we use the term puppy class throughout the book, we also encourage obedience training for adult dogs. Please visit my website at dianerosesolomon.com for more information on obedience training, pet care, pet safety and much more. If you have a specific behavioral concern be sure to contact a professional.

A note from Trainer Lyssa:

Trainer Lyssa says congratulations to you for being a responsible pet owner and taking your dog to puppy class. Trainer Lyssa is a real person and a highly qualified obedience trainer in San Diego, CA. Lyssa only uses positive dog training methods grounded in the scientific principles of animal behavioral learning. Also known as reward-based training, these humane techniques tap into dogs' natural motivations (food, play, praise, etc.) to quickly and painlessly change behavior.

The result? You get the well-mannered dog you want—while preserving trust and understanding between you and your dog.

Please visit her website at wholedogsports.com for more information on training as well as specialty and agility classes offered.

For more information about local trainers you can visit the Association of Professional Dog Trainers at: apdt.com/trainers/

Some tips to get you through the first few months:

1) Try to be home as much as possible, especially at first. If you work outside of the home, you can:

a. Crate train (but be sure to have someone let your dog out every few hours).

b. Utilize baby gates so that your dog can roam freely in a designated area.

2) Utilize a dog walker or a quality doggie day care in your area to socialize your dog.

3) Don't buy new furniture before you get a new dog, just in case.

4) Keep your shoes, socks, children's toys, food and anything else valuable closed in a closet. Puppies love to chew and can be quite destructive without proper boundaries. Trainer Lyssa suggests always having real chew bones from the pet store, to keep your puppy from chewing other things. This will keep their teeth clean too! Be sure to supervise any bone chewing.

5) Be sure to give your dog lots of long walks so that they have a chance to relieve themselves and burn off some of that puppy energy.

6) Never leave your dog chained up outside. It makes him vulnerable and scared. He can become lonely and potentially aggressive as a result. This is no way to treat your newest family member!

7) Never leave children unattended around your dog. Even the sweetest dogs can be provoked.

8) Teach children how to approach a dog they don't know. First, always ask a pet parent if it is ok to pet their dog. Then the dog should be allowed to sniff the back of your hand. You can ask where the dog likes to be pet, but it's always best to pet them under their chin where they can see your hand. Please see dogbiteprevention.org for more information.

Behavioral issues are one of the main reasons dogs are returned to shelters or breeders. Most of those dogs could be easily trained with patience. Dogs in New Zealand even learned how to drive. They really are trainable!

Thank you for doing your part and being responsible so that your new dog lives a happy life in your loving home. And remember, the puppy stage doesn't last very long so take lots of pictures!

Please check dianerosesolomon.com for more books in the "JJ" series coming soon!

About the author

Diane Rose-Solomon, a Certified Humane Education Specialist, rescued the real JJ 19 years ago. This is her second book in the JJ series, with three more books plus other interactive products and media in the works. Ms. Rose-Solomon lives in Los Angeles with her husband, two children and two rescued dogs, Gonzo and Ninja.

About the illustrator

Lisette Rotman is a graphic designer and artist living in New Jersey. She freelances for local start-ups and non-profit organizations. She loves her family's rescued kitties and plans to sell her artwork to raise money and awareness for animal groups. lisetteart.com